Hey NFL Fans!

You are no less than any Hall of Fame player! Every splash of color shows your love for the game! Pick up your crayons and let your creativity turn these NFL logos into vibrant masterpieces!

Happy Coloring 🎨🏈

- Year Established: 1960
- Conference: AFC West
- Mascot: K.C. Wolf
- Super Bowl Years: 1969, 2020, 2023, 2024
- Notable Players: Patrick Mahomes, Travis Kelce, Tyreek Hill, Derrick Thomas, Len Dawson
- Cool Fact: Arrowhead Stadium once set a record for being the loudest outdoor stadium.

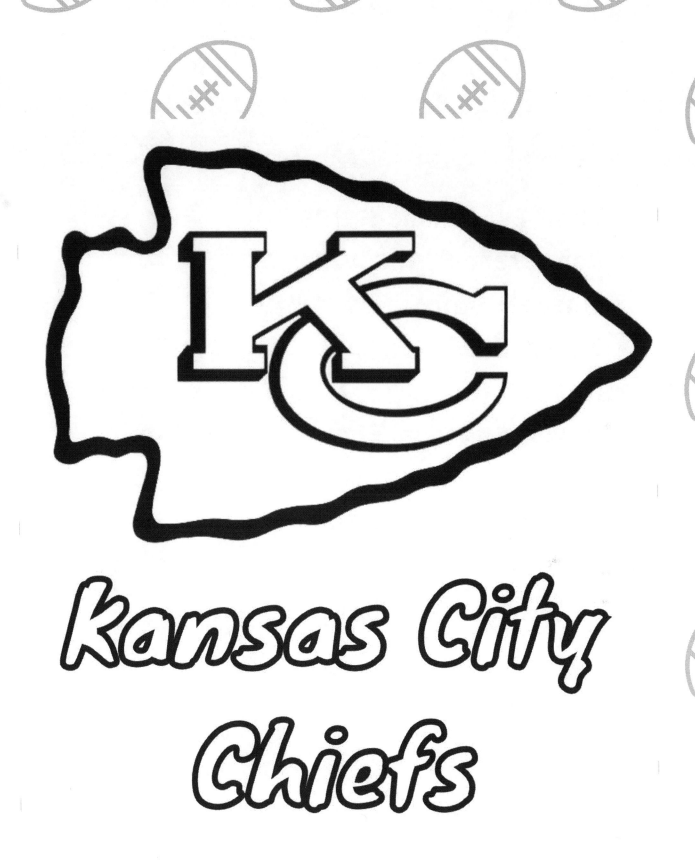

Kansas City Chiefs

- Year Established: 1960
- Conference: AFC West
- Mascot: Miles
- Super Bowl Years: 1998, 1999, 2016
- Notable Players: John Elway, Terrell Davis, Shannon Sharpe, Von Miller, Peyton Manning
- Cool Fact: The Broncos' home, Empower Field at Mile High, is known for its high elevation.

Denver
Broncos

- Year Established: 1960
- Conference: AFC West
- Mascot: Raider Rusher
- Super Bowl Years: 1977, 1981, 1984
- Notable Players: Marcus Allen, Ken Stabler, Howie Long, Tim Brown, Charles Woodson
- Cool Fact: The Raiders moved from Oakland to Las Vegas in 2020.

Las Vegas
Raiders

- Year Established: 1960
- Conference: AFC West
- Mascot: Boltman
- Super Bowl Years: None (Appearance: 1995)
- Notable Players: LaDainian Tomlinson, Junior Seau, Dan Fouts, Philip Rivers, Antonio Gates
- Cool Fact: The Chargers were originally based in Los Angeles, then moved to San Diego before returning to Los Angeles.

Los Angeles
Chargers

- Year Established: 1966
- Conference: AFC East
- Mascot: T.D.
- Super Bowl Years: 1972, 1973
- Notable Players: Dan Marino, Larry Csonka, Bob Griese, Jason Taylor, Zach Thomas
- Cool Fact: The Dolphins are the only team to have a perfect season, going 17-0 in 1972.

- Year Established: 1960
- Conference: AFC East
- Mascot: Pat Patriot
- Super Bowl Years: 2002, 2004, 2005, 2015, 2017, 2019
- Notable Players: Tom Brady, Rob Gronkowski, Julian Edelman, Ty Law, Tedy Bruschi
- Cool Fact: The Patriots have the most Super Bowl appearances in NFL history.

New England
Patriots

- Year Established: 1960
- Conference: AFC East
- Mascot: None (Unofficial: "J-E-T-S! Jets! Jets! Jets!" chant)
- Super Bowl Years: 1969
- Notable Players: Joe Namath, Curtis Martin, Don Maynard, Darrelle Revis, Joe Klecko
- Cool Fact: Joe Namath famously guaranteed the Jets' Super Bowl III win.

- Year Established: 1960
- Conference: AFC East
- Mascot: Billy Buffalo
- Super Bowl Years: None (Four consecutive appearances from 1991 to 1994)
- Notable Players: Jim Kelly, Thurman Thomas, Bruce Smith, Andre Reed, Josh Allen
- Cool Fact: The Bills are the only team to play in four consecutive Super Bowls.

- Year Established: 1976
- Conference: NFC West
- Mascot: Blitz, Boom, and Taima the Hawk
- Super Bowl Years: 2014
- Notable Players: Russell Wilson, Marshawn Lynch, Steve Largent, Richard Sherman, Walter Jones
- Cool Fact: The Seahawks' "12th Man" refers to their passionate fan base.

Seattle
Seahawks

- Year Established: 1898
- Conference: NFC West
- Mascot: Big Red
- Super Bowl Years: None
- Notable Players: Larry Fitzgerald, Pat Tillman, kurt Warner, Carson Palmer, J.J. Watt
- Cool Fact: The Cardinals are the oldest continuously run professional football team in the United States.

Arizona
Cardinals

- Year Established: 1936
- Conference: NFC West
- Mascot: Rampage
- Super Bowl Years: 2000, 2022
- Notable Players: Eric Dickerson, Aaron Donald, Kurt Warner, Marshall Faulk, Isaac Bruce
- Cool Fact: The Rams were the first NFL team to have a logo on their helmets.

Los Angeles
Rams

- Year Established: 1946
- Conference: NFC West
- Mascot: Sourdough Sam
- Super Bowl Years: 1982, 1985, 1989, 1990, 1995
- Notable Players: Joe Montana, Jerry Rice, Steve Young, Ronnie Lott, Frank Gore
- Cool Fact: The 49ers were named after the prospectors who arrived in Northern California during the 1849 Gold Rush.

San Francisco
49ers

- Year Established: 1933
- Conference: AFC North
- Mascot: Steely McBeam
- Super Bowl Years: 1975, 1976, 1979, 1980, 2006, 2009
- Notable Players: Terry Bradshaw, Joe Greene, Ben Roethlisberger, Troy Polamalu, Franco Harris
- Cool Fact: The Steelers have the most Super Bowl wins tied with the New England Patriots.

Pittsburgh Steelers

- Year Established: 1946
- Conference: AFC North
- Mascot: Chomps, Swagger
- Super Bowl Years: None
- Notable Players: Jim Brown, Otto Graham, Paul Warfield, Ozzie Newsome, Joe Thomas
- Cool Fact: The Browns are named after their original coach and co-founder, Paul Brown.

Cleveland
Browns

- Year Established: 1968
- Conference: AFC North
- Mascot: Who Dey
- Super Bowl Years: None (Appearances: 1982, 1989, 2022)
- Notable Players: Boomer Esiason, Chad Johnson, Ken Anderson, A.J. Green, Joe Burrow
- Cool Fact: The team was named after a previous Cincinnati football team that played from 1937 to 1941.

Cincinnati
Bengals

- Year Established: 1996
- Conference: AFC North
- Mascot: Poe
- Super Bowl Years: 2001, 2013
- Notable Players: Ray Lewis, Ed Reed, Joe Flacco, Lamar Jackson, Terrell Suggs
- Cool Fact: The team's name honors Edgar Allan Poe, a famous poet who lived in Baltimore.

Baltimore
Ravens

- Year Established: 1960
- Conference: NFC East
- Mascot: Rowdy
- Super Bowl Years: 1972, 1978, 1993, 1994, 1996
- Notable Players: Troy Aikman, Emmitt Smith, Michael Irvin, Roger Staubach, Tony Romo
- Cool Fact: The Cowboys are often called "America's Team" due to their wide fan base.

- Year Established: 1925
- Conference: NFC East
- Mascot: None (Unofficial: "NYG Man")
- Super Bowl Years: 1987, 1991, 2008, 2012
- Notable Players: Lawrence Taylor, Eli Manning, Michael Strahan, Frank Gifford, Phil Simms
- Cool Fact: The Giants are one of the five teams that joined the NFL in 1925.

New York
Giants

- Year Established: 1933
- Conference: NFC East
- Mascot: Swoop
- Super Bowl Years: 2018
- Notable Players: Reggie White, Brian Dawkins, Donovan McNabb, Carson Wentz, Nick Foles
- Cool Fact: The Eagles' victory in Super Bowl LII was their first-ever Super Bowl win.

Philadelphia
Eagles

- Year Established: 1932
- Conference: NFC East
- Mascot: None
- Super Bowl Years: 1983, 1988, 1992
- Notable Players: Joe Theismann, Art Monk, Darrell Green, John Riggins, Sean Taylor
- Cool Fact: The team officially changed its name to the Washington Commanders in 2022.

W

Washington Commanders

- Year Established: 1930
- Conference: NFC North
- Mascot: Roary
- Super Bowl Years: None
- Notable Players: Barry Sanders, Calvin Johnson, Matthew Stafford, Dick Lane, Lem Barney
- Cool Fact: The Lions host a game every year on Thanksgiving Day, a tradition dating back to 1934.

- Year Established: 1920
- Conference: NFC North
- Mascot: Staley Da Bear
- Super Bowl Years: 1986
- Notable Players: Walter Payton, Mike Ditka, Dick Butkus, Brian Urlacher, Gale Sayers
- Cool Fact: The Bears have one of the oldest and most storied histories in the NFL.

- Year Established: 1919
- Conference: NFC North
- Mascot: None (Unofficial: "Packers Fans" or "Cheeseheads")
- Super Bowl Years: 1967, 1968, 1997, 2011
- Notable Players: Bart Starr, Brett Favre, Aaron Rodgers, Reggie White, Ray Nitschke
- Cool Fact: The Packers are the only community-owned team in the NFL.

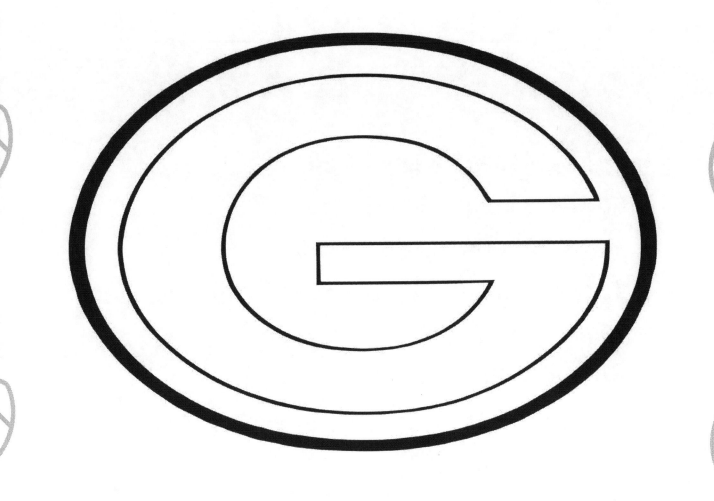

Green Bay
Packers

- Year Established: 1961
- Conference: NFC North
- Mascot: Viktor the Viking
- Super Bowl Years: None (Appearances: 1970, 1974, 1975, 1977)
- Notable Players: Fran Tarkenton, Randy Moss, Adrian Peterson, Cris Carter, Alan Page
- Cool Fact: The Vikings' horn sound is one of the most iconic stadium sounds in the NFL.

Minnesota Vikings

- Year Established: 1965
- Conference: NFC South
- Mascot: Freddie Falcon
- Super Bowl Years: None (Appearances: 1999, 2017)
- Notable Players: Matt Ryan, Julio Jones, Deion Sanders, Michael Vick, Tony Gonzalez
- Cool Fact: The Falcons were the first NFL team in the Deep South.

Atlanta Falcons

- Year Established: 1976
- Conference: NFC South
- Mascot: Captain Fear
- Super Bowl Years: 2003, 2021
- Notable Players: Derrick Brooks, Warren Sapp, Mike Alstott, Tom Brady, John Lynch
- Cool Fact: The Buccaneers won their second Super Bowl with Tom Brady in his first season with the team.

Tampa Bay Buccaneers

- Year Established: 1995
- Conference: NFC South
- Mascot: Sir Purr
- Super Bowl Years: None (Appearances: 2004, 2016)
- Notable Players: Cam Newton, Steve Smith, Luke Kuechly, Julius Peppers, Thomas Davis
- Cool Fact: The team's name reflects the powerful and stealthy nature of the panther.

Carolina
Panthers

- Year Established: 1967
- Conference: NFC South
- Mascot: Gumbo, Sir Saint
- Super Bowl Years: 2010
- Notable Players: Drew Brees, Alvin Kamara, Michael Thomas, Archie Manning, Rickey Jackson
- Cool Fact: The Saints' first winning season was not until their 21st season in 1987.

New Orleans
Saints

- Year Established: 2002
- Conference: AFC South
- Mascot: Toro
- Super Bowl Years: None
- Notable Players: J.J. Watt, Andre Johnson, Deshaun Watson, Arian Foster, DeAndre Hopkins
- Cool Fact: The Texans are the youngest franchise in the NFL.

Houston
Texans

- Year Established: 1953
- Conference: AFC South
- Mascot: Blue
- Super Bowl Years: 1971, 2007
- Notable Players: Peyton Manning, Johnny Unitas, Marvin Harrison, Edgerrin James, Reggie Wayne
- Cool Fact: The Colts were originally based in Baltimore before moving to Indianapolis in 1984.

Indianapolis Colts

- Year Established: 1995
- Conference: AFC South
- Mascot: Jaxson de Ville
- Super Bowl Years: None
- Notable Players: Fred Taylor, Tony Boselli, Maurice Jones-Drew, Mark Brunell, Jalen Ramsey
- Cool Fact: The Jaguars' home stadium features one of the largest video boards in the world.

Jacksonville

Jaguars

- Year Established: 1960 (as Houston Oilers)
- Conference: AFC South
- Mascot: T-Rac
- Super Bowl Years: None (Appearance: 2000)
- Notable Players: Steve McNair, Eddie George, Warren Moon, Chris Johnson, Derrick Henry
- Cool Fact: The team was originally the Houston Oilers before relocating to Tennessee and becoming the Titans.

Tennessee
Titans

Made in United States
Orlando, FL
22 December 2024

56352056R00037